How Can Objects Move?

HOUGHTON MIFFLIN HARCOURT

behind

in front of

We use these words to tell where it is.

How do we tell where something is?

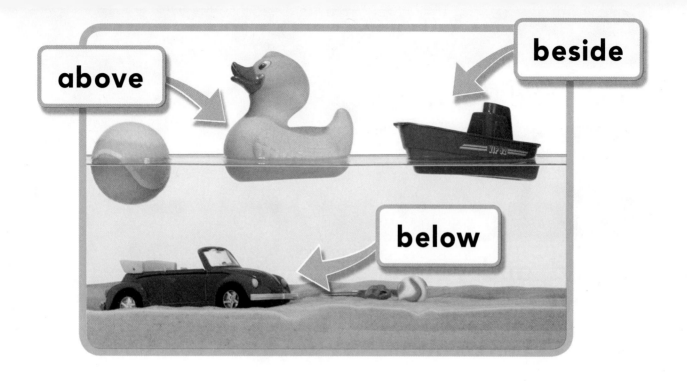

above

beside

below

We use these words, too.

back and forth

round and round

We use these words to tell how things move.

How do we tell how something moves?

zigzag

down

up

fast

straight

Things can move round and round. They can move straight or in a zigzag.

attract

magnet

Magnets attract, or pull, some objects.

How can magnets move objects?

magnet

steel door

They pull objects made from iron or steel.

Moving Lines

Ask children to form a single line and hold hands. Lead them in different movements around the room. For example, guide them to make a zigzag line as they walk.

Name Positions

Arrange three to five children in a group formation. Help children use one another's names to orally complete the sentences below. If possible, take a picture of the children in formation and distribute a copy to each child. Then have children complete the sentences to go with the picture.

_____ is beside _____.

_____ is above _____.

_____ is below _____.

_____ is behind _____.

_____ is in front of _____.

Vocabulary	
above	in front of
attract	magnets
back and forth	round and round
behind	straight
below	up and down
beside	zigzag